AMERICAN SPACE MISSIONS

ASTRONAUTS, EXPLORATION, AND DISCOVERY

The Coolest Job in the Universe

Working Aboard the International Space Station

Henry M. Holden

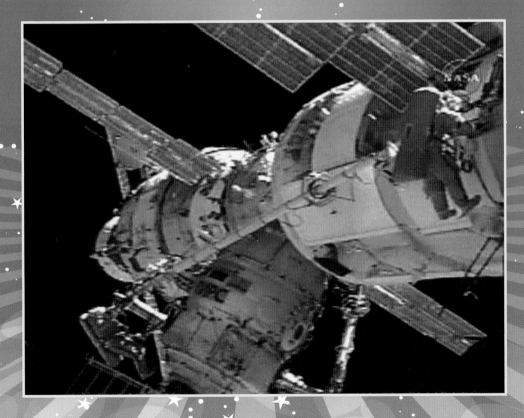

Enslow Publishers, Inc.
40 Industrial Road
Box 398
Berkeley Heights, NJ 07922
USA
http://www.enslow.com

Original edition published as *Living and Working Aboard the International Space Station* in 2004.

Library of Congress Cataloging-in-Publication Data

Holden, Henry M.
  The coolest job in the universe : working aboard the International Space Station / Henry M. Holden.
    p. cm. — (American space missions—astronauts, exploration, and discovery)
  Includes bibliographical references and index.
  Summary: "Explores the International Space Station (ISS), including its construction and the missions required to build it, living and working aboard the ISS, and its importance as the future of the space program"—Provided by publisher.
  ISBN 978-0-7660-4074-8
  1. International Space Station—Juvenile literature. 2. Space sciences—Research—Juvenile literature. 3. Manned space flight—Juvenile literature. I. Title.
  TL797.15.H648 2013
  629.44'2—dc23
                    2012002222
Future editions:
Paperback ISBN 978-1-4644-0077-3
ePUB ISBN 978-1-4645-0984-1
PDF ISBN 978-1-4646-0984-8

Printed in the United States of America
022013 Lake Book Manufacturing, Inc., Melrose Park, IL
10 9 8 7 6 5 4 3 2

To Our Readers: We have done our best to make sure all Internet addresses in this book were active and appropriate when we went to press. However, the author and the publisher have no control over and assume no liability for the material available on those Internet sites or on other Web sites they may link to. Any comments or suggestions can be sent by e-mail to comments@enslow.com or to the address on the back cover.

♻ Enslow Publishers, Inc., is committed to printing our books on recycled paper. The paper in every book contains 10% to 30% post-consumer waste (PCW). The cover board on the outside of each book contains 100% PCW. Our goal is to do our part to help young people and the environment too!

Illustration Credits: AP Images / *Houston Chronicle*, Smiley N. Pool, p. 29; AP Images / NASA, pp. 4–5, 24, 32; AP Images / NASA TV, pp. 1, 8; AP Images / Orbital Sciences, p. 41; NASA, pp. 13, 14, 19, 21, 27, 34, 37, 38; NASA Johnson Space Center, pp. 16, 22; NASA Kennedy Space Center, p. 10; NASA Orbital Debris Program Office, p. 7.

Cover Illustration: NASA / STS-119 Shuttle Crew (A view of the International Space Station from the space shuttle *Discovery* on April 6, 2009).

Contents

Danger in Space

It was Sunday, October 24, 1999. The U.S. Space Command, near Colorado Springs, Colorado, was watching two objects on its radar. The objects, the International Space Station (ISS) and the remains of a Pegasus rocket, were screaming toward each other at a combined speed of almost 35,000 miles (56,327 kilometers) per hour. If they collided, the space

station would be destroyed. The piece of rocket had been drifting in space for many years, unable to return to Earth. The ISS had only been in orbit for about a year. Space Command predicted that the two would pass less than a mile apart. That was a serious threat to the ISS. Ground controllers remotely fired small engines on the ISS and changed its orbit slightly to prevent a possible collision with the old rocket.[1]

Space Junk

As of 2011, the Joint Space Operations Center is monitoring 22,000 man-made orbiting objects.[2] This debris includes thousands of nuts, bolts, gloves, old satellites, and other debris from space missions. It forms an orbiting garbage dump around Earth. More than two hundred objects, most of them trash bags, were released by the *Mir* space station.[3] The *Mir* station had been Russia's first space station. No one knows exactly how much debris is out there. At least one piece destroyed a satellite. In 1996, a French satellite collided with a fragment of a rocket that had exploded in space ten years earlier. The impact sent the satellite spinning out of control.[4]

There are other objects, too small to be tracked from Earth, speeding through space. Small flecks of paint can damage a cockpit window on a space shuttle. For example, a tiny speck of paint from a satellite dug a pit in a space shuttle window almost a quarter-inch (.64 centimeters) wide.[5] "We get hit regularly on the shuttle," said Joseph Loftus, a NASA engineer, in September 2000. "We've replaced more than eighty [shuttle] windows because of debris impacts."[6]

More than 22,000 objects larger than 4 inches (10 centimeters) are currently tracked by the U.S. Space Surveillance Network. Only about 1,000 of these represent operational spacecraft; the rest are orbital debris. The estimated population of particles between .4 inches and 4 inches (1 to 10 centimeters) in diameter is approximately 500,000.[7] Fortunately, much of this debris will eventually burn up, falling back to Earth.

This computer-generated image shows objects in Earth orbit that NASA is currently tracking. About 95 percent of the objects shown in the image as white dots are space junk.

In this image from **NASA TV,** space station commander Pavel Vinogradov (right) and astronaut Jeff Williams (left) prepare to replace a camera on the outside of the ISS during a spacewalk on June 1, 2006. The ISS can be a dangerous place to work, especially when astronauts perform spacewalks.

The ISS can be a dangerous place to work. Dust-sized meteorites can be a risk to spacewalking astronauts. The particles whiz by at 17,500 miles (28,163 kilometers) per hour. These tiny objects are traveling faster than a bullet. To protect themselves, astronauts wear space suits that act like bulletproof clothing. The suits are made of layers of Kevlar, Teflon, and aluminum Mylar. Any hole or tear in the space suit could cause a rapid and fatal decompression. However, the risk to the astronauts is low because they are such small objects in space. Still, to lower the risk, they do not stay outside the ISS for extended periods.

Despite a close call on June 28, 2011, the ISS has not yet been damaged by space junk. Even so, NASA takes the risk seriously. Its astronauts reinforce the station's most vulnerable parts during construction.

The space shuttle *Endeavour* is suspended in a vertical position inside the Vehicle Assembly Building at Kennedy Space Center on October 15, 1998. *Endeavour* was the first space shuttle flight for the assembly of the International Space Station.

CHAPTER 2

Building the International Space Station

Human space flight began in 1961. At first, the flights were short, but as humans learned more about space, the flights grew longer and longer. In November 2003, the International Space Station marked a milestone in space history. Humans had lived continuously in orbit for three years.

The International Space Station is the most ambitious engineering project in human history and the largest spacecraft ever put in orbit. The United States, the United Kingdom, the Netherlands, Russia, France, Germany, Italy, Canada, Japan, Belgium, Norway, Denmark, Brazil, Sweden, Switzerland, and Spain are all helping by either supplying parts or astronauts. When finished, the station's internal volume will be about the size of one 747-jet passenger compartment.[1] The ISS is designed to provide pressurized living and working space for a crew of up to seven.

Construction

Parts for the ISS are carried in the cargo bay of the space shuttles. It will take about 160 spacewalks to assemble the ISS. When finished, it will be 361 feet (110 meters) wide, 290 feet (88 meters) long, about 14 stories high, and it will weigh about 500 tons (about 1 million pounds).[2]

The ISS has three main sections. They are research modules, service modules, and living or habitation modules. Russia launched the first section of the ISS, the Zarya module, in November 1998. It provided the initial power and propulsion. The United States space shuttle *Endeavour* carried the U.S.-built 12-ton (26,880 pounds, 12,193 kilograms) Unity connecting module about two weeks later. These two modules had never been connected and had to fit perfectly the first time. *Endeavour's* crew successfully attached the modules during the twelve-day mission.[3] A third section, Zvezda, joined up with the station in July 2000. Zvezda provided living quarters and life-support systems. Destiny, the United States science laboratory, was attached in February 2001.

Expedition One

On October 31, 2000, astronaut William Shepherd and cosmonauts Yuri Gidzenko and Sergei Krikalev flew to the station on a Russian *Soyuz* rocket. They became the ISS's first full-time crew. Krikalev served as the flight engineer, responsible for the systems. Shepherd served as the expedition commander, and Gidzenko served as the *Soyuz* commander.[4] The crew lived on the ISS for four months. However, before they arrived, three space shuttle crews visited the ISS, stocking it with supplies and equipment.

Russia launched the first section of the ISS, the Zarya module, in November 1998, and the United States sent the second module, Unity, aboard *Endeavour* a couple weeks later. This photo taken from *Endeavour* provides a view of the connected Zarya and Unity modules after the space shuttle released them from its cargo bay.

Bulletproof Skin

Each of the ISS's living and research modules has to be lifted into orbit. To keep their weight low, they are made of aluminum. To protect the crew from micrometeoroids, these modules wear "bulletproof

The first full-time crew of the International Space Station, flight engineer Sergei Krikalev (left), expedition commander William Shepherd (center), and *Soyuz* commander Yuri Gidzenko, pose for this photo shortly before their space flight to the ISS. The three men are sporting the space suits they wore for the *Soyuz* mission.

vests," or micrometeoroid debris shields. These are made from layers of Kevlar, ceramic fabrics, and other materials and surround each of the aluminum modules.

Robots and Sky Walkers

As parts of the ISS are placed in orbit, they must be attached to the station. Robotic arms do some of this work. The space shuttle's mechanical arm and several ISS arms operate as "space cranes" moving the parts into place. Spacewalking astronauts do most of the assembly. They use special tools, wear pressurized suits, and use tethers to hook themselves to the ISS. Even though an astronaut wears a thruster backpack any time he or she is outside the station, walking in space is dangerous.[5] "When we do a spacewalk without the presence of a docked space shuttle, drifting away would be a fatal mistake," said ISS science officer Don Pettit.[6] Astronauts could also be hit by micrometeorites. This is why NASA built the Robonaut.

Robonaut

Robonaut is a humanoid robot that performs some work outside the ISS. Robonaut1 was built but never made it to space. Robonaut2 was launched in February 2011.

Robonaut is about the size of an astronaut in a space suit. It has flexible arms and gloves, complete with five fingers. The gloves have sensors and act the way a human hand does.[7] Robonaut's hand works with small tools, such as tweezers and common handheld tools.[8] Its head has two color cameras for stereoscopic eyes. This means it can

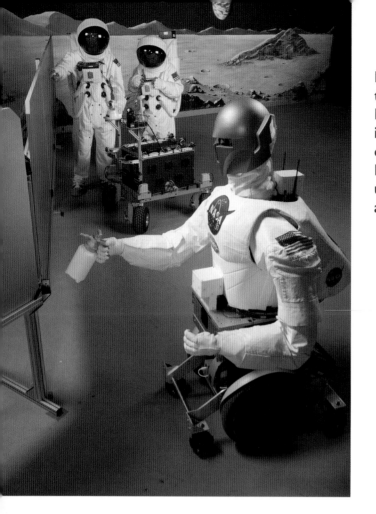

Robonaut performs a mock training exercise at the Ames Research Center. First used in February 2011, Robonaut carries out tasks outside the International Space Station under the control of an astronaut inside the ISS.

see in three dimensions. Its "skin" is a woven material similar to the space-suit fabric. The skin protects vulnerable areas against radiation and the extreme temperatures in space.[9]

Robonaut is under the control of an astronaut inside the ISS. Wearing special gloves and a headset, the astronaut has virtual-reality eyes and hands. He or she will communicate with Robonaut using a remote camera and monitor. Since its head is too small, Robonaut has its "brain" in its chest area. It cannot think like humans, handle complex tasks, or replace the decision-making abilities of human astronauts.

During spacewalks, astronauts devote about one-third of their time to tasks, such as installing foot restraints and laying out tools. These are routine jobs for Robonaut.[10]

Solar Power

Electrical power is an important resource on the ISS. It allows the crew to live and work comfortably. Computers run almost everything on the ISS, and they use a lot of electricity. The only readily available source of energy for the ISS is solar energy from the sun. The ISS converts this energy to electrical power using a process called photovoltaics.

More than a quarter million silicon solar cells, mounted on eight large solar arrays, gather the solar energy.[11] The solar cells convert sunlight into electricity in the same way solar cells power a handheld calculator. The solar panels rotate so they face the sun as the station orbits Earth. However, when the ISS is in Earth's shadow, batteries supply power for the station. During the sunlit part of the orbit, the batteries are recharged. When the station is completed, the solar arrays will be as large as one football field.[12] They will generate enough energy to power fifty-five houses.[13]

The concept of a space station is not new. Jonathan Swift wrote about the city of Laputa in his book *Gulliver's Travels*, which was published in 1726. Swift's city moved between Earth and the sky by magnetism.

CHAPTER 3

The First Space Stations

The International Space Station is not the first space station. In 1971, the Soviet Union launched *Salyut 1* to study the physical, biological, and psychological effects of weightlessness. The first crew, aboard a *Soyuz 10* rocket, attempted to dock with *Salyut* twice, but the hatch would not open. The mission failed, and the crew returned home. The next crew docked successfully and lived on the station for twenty-four days.[1]

A tragic accident occurred during the crew's return trip. A valve on *Soyuz* accidentally opened when it separated from *Salyut,* moments before the *Soyuz* was going to descend. The valve would normally open as the spacecraft descended, equalizing the pressure inside and outside the spacecraft. Having the valve open too early in space was fatal. When the rescue team located the spacecraft, the crew was dead.

In 1975, the *Apollo-Soyuz* mission was the first space flight conducted jointly by the United States and the Soviet Union. The two spacecrafts

The first space flight conducted jointly by the United States and the Soviet Union was the *Apollo-Soyuz* mission in 1975. In this photo, the crew is shown from left to right: American astronauts Deke Slayton, Tom Stafford, and Vance Brand, and Soviet cosmonauts Aleksey Leonov and Valeri Kubasov.

docked and conducted experiments. The two countries were still bitter rivals at that time. Yet, they worked together in peace.

In 1982, the *Cosmos 1267* docked to *Salyut 6*. This was an important step in the development of the ISS. It proved that large vehicles could dock to a space station.

Salyut 7 was the last of the Soviet space stations before the *Mir* modular space station.[2] It remained in orbit for about nine years.

Skylab

In 1973, the United States launched *Skylab*, its first manned space station. Weighing nearly one hundred tons, *Skylab* was the converted third stage of a Saturn-V rocket. It had two solar panels to supply power.

By now, scientists understood that exercise was important in space. *Skylab* had an exercise bike and a docking port with air locks. This allowed the crew to make spacewalks. Astronauts conducted more than three hundred experiments during the eight months they lived on board. Scientists learned about astronomy in ways that are impossible from Earth. Because *Skylab* orbited above Earth's atmosphere, there were no clouds or pollution to block the telescopes. *Skylab* proved that humans could live in space for long periods of time. The last crew returned to Earth in 1974. Five years later, the abandoned spacecraft burned up on reentry.

Russian *Mir*

Mir was launched in 1986. The first expansion module, Kvant, was added in 1987. With this addition, *Mir* became the world's first modular space station. It was composed of different modules attached to docking ports. Together, these modules made a larger station. *Mir* looked like a giant dragonfly with its wings outstretched.[3] Astronaut Jerry Linenger compared *Mir* to "six school buses all hooked together."[4] Other astronauts believe that *Mir* resembled a giant insect.

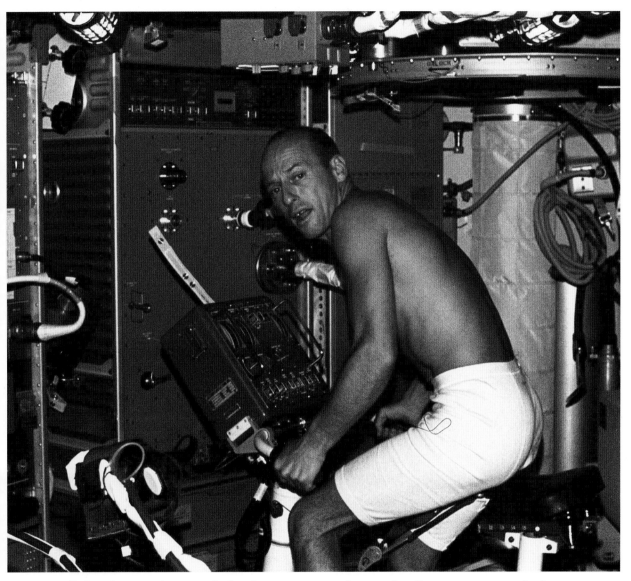

Scientists understood the importance of exercise for astronauts during space missions. In this photo, *Skylab 2* commander Charles Conrad, Jr., uses the exercise bike in the crew quarters of *Skylab*.

In this 1993 photo, the American space shuttle *Atlantis* is docked with the Russian space station *Mir*. Together, American and Russian scientists conducted experiments using *Mir* as a test site for future space stations.

Americans Dock With *Mir*

On June 29, 1995, America's space shuttles began docking with *Mir*. American and Russian scientists conducted experiments using *Mir* as a test bed for future space stations. Researchers performed tests that would help them build the ISS.[5] The space shuttle docked nine times with *Mir*, and astronauts from twelve different nations lived on *Mir* over the years.[6] Astronauts aboard *Mir* even grew the first crop of wheat in outer space.

Mir remained in orbit for fifteen years, three times longer than planned. As *Mir* grew older, it became more accident-prone. In February 1997, there was a fire on the station. There were computer malfunctions and power failures. In June 1997, a nearly fatal collision with the Russian supply rocket put a hole in the station, almost killing the crew.

In June 1998, *Mir* shut down. The empty spacecraft burned up on reentry in March 2001.[7] *Mir*'s end coincided with the first successful U.S.-Russian expedition to the International Space Station.

With the ISS in orbit, life became a little more comfortable for space-station crew members. The ISS is larger than *Mir*, and scientists knew more about living in space.

Despite the hostile environment of space, astronauts working aboard the International Space Station enjoy some Earthlike living conditions, including clean air, food, and water. In this photo, three astronauts test out the station's new recycling system as they prepare to drink purified water.

Home Sweet Space Station

Space is the most hostile environment for humans to live and work. It is cold, and there is no air to breathe or water to drink. However, living inside the International Space Station is almost like being on Earth. There is clean air, water, and food.

To maintain an orbit, the space station travels at 17,500 miles (28,163.5 kilometers) per hour, or about 5 miles (8 kilometers) per second. If you could bring the station down to 1,000 feet (305 meters) at this speed, it could travel from the west coast of the United States to the east coast in about nine minutes.[1]

Microgravity

Gravity is what keeps our feet on the ground. Anytime we drop or throw something, we are watching gravity in action. On Earth, our feet are pulled to the ground by one "g" of gravity. Scientists believe gravity causes plants to root into the ground and encourages fluids to mix. On the ISS, gravity is only a small fraction of that on Earth. This is called microgravity, or "zero-g." Sometimes it is called weightlessness. Microgravity describes this very weak gravitational effect.

Because of gravity, all artificial satellites like the ISS try to fall back to Earth. If a person on the ISS drops a pencil, it floats because the ISS, the person, and the pencil, are all in free fall toward Earth. Because there is this gravitational pull on the ISS, small engines on the ISS need to be used to reboost it to its proper orbit.

Humans in Microgravity

In microgravity, a person's muscles and bones do not work as hard as they do on Earth. On the ISS, the crew must exercise or their muscles will atrophy, or weaken, and their bones will lose density. The only known way to reduce bone-density loss is to place stress on the bones. Astronauts must exercise two hours every day. This may include running on a modified treadmill, riding a stationary bike, or using a "weightlifting" device that uses rubber bands instead of iron weights.[2] There are other health issues in microgravity. Wounds heal more slowly, and the immune system weakens. Scientists do not yet know why.

Artificial Gravity

In the 1950s, rocket pioneer Wernher von Braun envisioned a wheel-shaped space station that would spin like a carnival ride. The spinning would create a centrifugal force. That force would create artificial gravity. This idea was not practical at that time, but scientists adapted his idea to help today's astronauts.[3] Scientists are developing a small, human-powered centrifuge. An astronaut pedals a bike around a 360-degree circle. Depending on the speed the astronaut is going and the size of the track, he or she will experience some artificial gravity.[4] This may help prevent bone-density loss and would be a great benefit for astronauts on longer-duration missions, such as to Mars.

Astronauts on the ISS must learn to live and work in microgravity. In this photo, astronaut Michael Gernhardt floats upside down in the Quest Airlock prior to suiting up for a spacewalk to work on the exterior of the ISS.

Return to Earth

Gravity pulls blood and fluids toward the lower body and feet. In microgravity, the fluids move to the upper body, neck, and head. It can cause some astronauts to get puffy faces. There are receptors in the carotid arteries in the neck that sense this extra fluid. The body's natural response is to eliminate this fluid. On reentry, gravity pulls the fluids back down to the astronaut's feet, leaving less in the brain. The body has eliminated what it sensed to be excess fluid. As a result, the astronauts must drink a combination of water and salt tablets, a hypotonic solution like a sports drink, or they will get dizzy or black out.[5]

The Neutral Buoyancy Laboratory

Part of an astronaut's training is to learn how to move safely in microgravity. The 6.2-million-gallon Neutral Buoyancy Laboratory (NBL) is four stories deep. It allows astronauts to safely practice the movements they will use during a spacewalk. The large tank contains a mock-up of the shuttle's payload bay. Astronauts simulate setting up antennas and testing the use of foot restraints and handholds. They wear underwater versions of space suits and are made neutrally buoyant by attaching floats and weights to their suits, until they neither rise nor fall in the tank.[6] For every hour the astronaut expects to walk in space, he or she will practice for about ten hours in the NBL.[7]

Astronaut Rex Walheim is aided by divers as he works with astronaut Mike Fossum in a mock-up of the space shuttle's payload bay during a spacewalk exercise at the Neutral Buoyancy Laboratory (NBL) on March 10, 2011. Astronauts train at the NBL to prepare for life in microgravity aboard the ISS.

Conserving Water and Oxygen in Space

Because water is in short supply on the ISS, almost every drop is recycled. Each crew member is allowed only about forty-three ounces of water—a little more than a quart—per day.[8] The crews do not take showers, because the floating water bubbles would bounce around. Instead, they take sponge baths. They wash their hair with dry shampoo and wipe it off with a damp towel. The water recycling system reclaims water from the hydrogen fuel cells, toothbrushing, hand washing, the crew's breath, and even from the toilet. Laboratory animals even have their breath and urine recycled.[9] The air-conditioning system condenses the moisture from the air and purifies it. Without careful recycling, 5,000 gallons of water would have to be resupplied from Earth each year.[10]

The oxygen people breathe on Earth comes from green plants, algae, and phytoplankton, through a process called photosynthesis. When plants are exposed to light, they convert carbon dioxide and water into glucose and oxygen. Although there are green plants for experiments on the ISS, there are not enough to make breathable air. Most of the station's oxygen comes from a process called "electrolysis." This process uses electricity from the solar panels to split water molecules into hydrogen and oxygen gases. Astronauts breathe the oxygen, and the hydrogen is vented into space.[11]

Personal Satellite Assistant

There are many tasks for the crew aboard the ISS. They must monitor the amount of oxygen, carbon dioxide, and other gases in the air. They will even measure bacterial growth, air temperature, and air pressure.

Scientists decided that a small mobile robot could perform these same tasks. The Personal Satellite Assistant (PSA) is a small intelligent robot that will serve as another set of eyes, ears, and nose for the ISS crew.[12] About the size of a softball, the PSA will have sensors to monitor the environment. It will have a camera for video conferencing, navigation sensors, and wireless network connections. It will even move under its own power, so it can zip around the spacecraft.[13]

Eating and Sleeping in Space

Astronauts use sleeping bags to restrain themselves while they sleep so they do not float around. On the ISS, there are crew quarters for each member of the expedition's crew, with six "sleep stations." Each is large enough for just one person. Inside each crew cabin is a sleeping bag and a large window to look out into space. The crew uses sleep masks when they sleep. Otherwise, they would see the sun rise and set every ninety minutes. The sunlight entering the window is enough to disturb a sleeper who is not wearing a sleep mask. They also use earplugs to block out noises from fans, pumps, and equipment.

Sometimes, the ISS hosts visiting crew. Visiting astronauts, if it is okay with the commander, can sleep anywhere in the ISS, as long as they attach themselves to something and the area is well-ventilated.

In this photo, three astronauts rest in their sleeping bags, which are secured to the middeck of the space shuttle *Discovery* while it is docked with the ISS. Securing the sleeping bags prevents the astronauts from floating around while they sleep.

Even though engineers have tried to make the environment on board the ISS as close to Earthlike as possible, the crew has major adjustments to make. The ISS has personal-hygiene stations where the crew can wash and use the toilet. The toilets are similar to those in an airliner, except they have foot restraints and seat belts. Instead of the bio-wastes being flushed away with water, they are swept away with a suction system. These wastes are not dumped overboard. They are dried, stored, and taken back to Earth on the shuttle.

The early *Mercury* and *Gemini* astronauts had to eat bite-sized food-cubes covered with gelatin, to prevent crumbs. In microgravity, crumbs are dangerous because they float and can get into the equipment. The food is much better now. Along with a refrigerator, the crew has a microwave oven, and they eat shrimp cocktail, steak, and chicken salsa.[14]

The ISS gets all its food from the space shuttle or Russia's *Progress* cargo spacecraft. Some of the food is dried, and then water is added to it at mealtime. Most of the food is packed in pouches and ready to eat, either cold or heated. Fresh fruit, veggies, milk, and ice cream are shipped up to the ISS on the space shuttles and *Progress* cargo spacecraft.

Taking Out the Trash

Since there are no clothes washers or dryers on board the ISS, the crews dress in "disposable" clothing. When the clothing is dirty, they throw it away. Trash, such as food packages, human waste, and solid waste from science projects, is not easy to recycle. Still, someone has to take out the trash. The shuttle and *Progress* do this job. Every shuttle that brings up fresh supplies turns into a trash truck. When it leaves, it takes many sealed trash bags back to Earth. Since the Russian *Progress* craft does not carry a crew, it gets rid of trash in a more exciting way. After its cargo is unloaded, the trash bags are loaded aboard. Then *Progress* is shut tight, and it heads back to Earth. As it reenters Earth's atmosphere, it heats up and catches fire. Both the spacecraft and all the trash burn up in the atmosphere.

Cosmonaut Yury Onufrienko is photographed on the ISS with apples and oranges floating in front of him. Most of the food that astronauts eat on the ISS is dried or packed in pouches that can be eaten cold or heated. However, the crew does get some fresh fruit and vegetables.

Wiping Out Germs

Microbes were the first things to live on the ISS. They came from Earth, carried on by parts of the ISS and by the crews who assembled the ISS. These tiny microbes are viruses, bacteria, and fungi. These "bugs" now live on the surfaces of the ISS, on the systems, and in the astronauts' bodies. Scientists have found that microbes grow rapidly in microgravity. If not controlled, they could make the crew sick.

The crews' own bodies keep most of the germs under control. Other microbes are removed by the station's air- and water-cleaning systems. Still, the astronauts have to fight the microbes that could cause harm. Their daily duties include wiping surfaces in their work and living areas with cloths that have a germ-killing liquid on them.

Radiation in Space

Earth's atmosphere filters out most of the dangerous radiation from space. However, when astronauts travel outside the atmosphere, they are exposed to this radiation. Scientists have developed some protection against this radiation. It is found in hydrogen compounds. One material that is lightweight and contains hydrogen is polyethylene. A three-inch shield of polyethylene will block about 35 percent of the radiation throughout the interior of the station. Astronauts also take large doses of vitamins A and C to help absorb the radiation-produced particles in their bodies.[15]

Lifeboat in Space

Like a ship at sea, the ISS needs a lifeboat. If the crew has to abandon the ISS, a crew return vehicle is needed. Currently, a Russian *Soyuz* spacecraft that can carry three crew members is docked to ISS to serve as a lifeboat.

The ISS will serve as a long-term research platform to help us learn ways to improve and preserve life on Earth. On the ISS, scientists will perform experiments not possible on Earth.

CHAPTER 5

Research on the International Space Station

The International Space Station is useful for growing and experimenting with proteins, enzymes, bacteria, and viruses. In microgravity, bacteria and cancer cells grow larger and looser shapes. Scientists can study their growth more easily and perhaps get a better understanding of the basic building blocks of life.[1] The knowledge from these experiments may help doctors develop new drugs. Cultures grown in the ISS may be used to test new treatments for cancer without risking harm to the patients.[2] The ongoing research might lead to cures for diabetes and other serious illnesses. The research may also lead to a way to grow human tissues and possibly to create new organs.[3]

In space, the body loses calcium, a mineral necessary for strong bones, at a rate of nearly one percent a month. Without gravity to put a load on the skeleton, air molecules in bones expand. This decreases the bone's density, and the bones dissolve away. Astronaut David Wolf, who flew two shuttle missions, spent more than 143 days in space.

Russian cosmonaut Sergei Volkov examines the progress of a new growth experiment in the greenhouse kept in the payload bay of the International Space Station. The ISS provides a useful workspace for experimenting with proteins, enzymes, bacteria, and viruses.

He lost about 13 percent of the bone mineral in his pelvis.[4] Scientists are searching for ways to prevent this.

In twenty or thirty years, we may send people to Mars or beyond. In October 1989, NASA launched the unmanned *Galileo* spacecraft to Jupiter, the next planet beyond Mars. It arrived more than five years later.[5] Before humans can make such a trip, we must learn how very long periods of microgravity affect the body. Astronauts are using the ISS for these studies.

Scientists are growing zeolite crystals on the ISS. Among other useful things, these crystals absorb hydrogen. Scientists hope one day

The ISS allows scientists to study Earth's climate from beyond our atmosphere. This photo of Hurricane Irene was taken by a crew member aboard the ISS on August 26, 2011, as the storm approached the southeastern United States.

to replace gasoline-burning cars with hydrogen-burning cars. These zeolite crystals may one day be used to line the fuel tank in place of gasoline. The hydrogen stored in the crystals would power the car.[6]

Earth Science

The ISS allows us to study Earth's climate from outside the atmosphere. Scientists study large-scale, long-term changes in the environment. They are able to forecast weather more accurately and provide early warning of hurricanes and other violent storms. They are also able to study the effects of air pollution, such as smog over cities, water pollution, and oil spills. From the ISS, they have a worldwide view not available on the ground.

Some experiments take place outside the ISS in outer space. These study long-term exposure to radiation, micrometeoroids, and the extreme temperatures of space. These studies may lead to better planning for long-distance space travel.

Flames burn differently in microgravity. In the absence of convection currents, in which warm air rises and cool air sinks, scientists can study the combustion process in ways not possible on Earth. The absence of convection allows scientists to study molten metals more thoroughly than on Earth. From these studies, scientists hope to create better metal alloys (substances made from two or more metals).

Someday, the ISS may be used as a base camp for future trips to the moon and the universe. It may also act as a dock for future spacecraft.

CHAPTER 6

Base Camp to the Universe

One day in the future, a space shuttle will dock with the International Space Station. The astronauts will transfer to a new type of spacecraft docked at the ISS that will explore the depths of space. The future spacecraft will need to be lightweight and propelled by a reliable source of energy. The strange spacecraft may look like a giant kite that travels on solar winds from the sun. The sails will be driven by photons—particles of energy emitted from sunlight.[1]

The ISS gives us endless visions and possibilities for exploring Earth's resources and the solar system. Humans may use it as a platform to launch future space colonies. One day it may be a space tourist stop. The ISS may act as a shipyard in space, where the vehicles that will explore deep space will be built. Someday people may use it as a base camp to mine asteroids for precious and rare metals. By exploring space, scientists hope to discover how life began. At 10 million miles per hour, about 250 times faster than our fastest spacecraft travels, a trip to the nearest star system would take three hundred years.[2] The ISS may serve as the base camp to explore the universe.

Columbia Disaster

On February 1, 2003, space shuttle *Columbia* broke up on reentry, killing all seven crew members on board. Mental-health counselors on the ground helped the three-member crew aboard the ISS deal with their

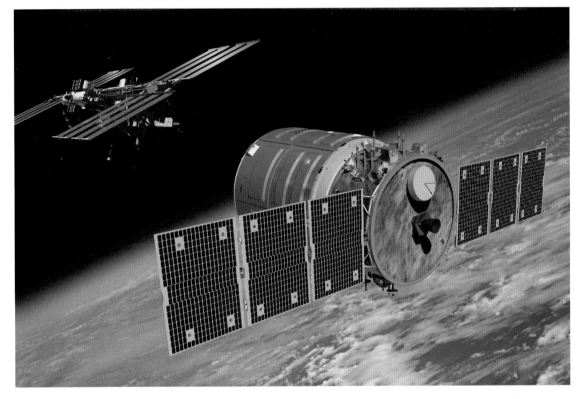

This artist's rendering by Orbital Sciences shows its proposed Cygnus spacecraft (right) as it approaches the International Space Station. The U.S. government ended the space shuttle program in July 2011, and NASA will be turning to private contractors to continue sending people and supplies to the ISS. This will open up opportunities for new space shuttles to fly into space and to even bring tourists to the ISS.

grief following the disaster. The crew members said their emotions over the loss of their seven friends on *Columbia* seemed to be greater in orbit, because they were isolated and so far away.[3]

NASA stopped all space-shuttle flights until the cause of the accident was known. This had a serious impact on building the ISS. The crew was supposed to switch in March on the shuttle *Atlantis*. With all shuttles grounded, a new plan was developed. The Russian *Progress* M–47 cargo craft would resupply the ISS with food and water until the shuttles were flying again. The three-man crew returned to Earth in June. NASA kept a two-person crew rotating every six months on the ISS.[4] These crews launched aboard a Russian *Soyuz* TMA–2 spacecraft until the shuttles returned to flight in 2005 with *Discovery*.[5] In 2010, President Barack Obama announced the extension of the ISS mission until 2020. However, NASA shuttles were stopped in 2011.

The astronauts who live on the ISS know there are risks from micrometeorites and radiation from the sun. Still, they feel the risks are worth it. Astronaut Andy Allen said, "I know spaceflight is a risk, and I know I may not come back from a flight . . . the risk of losing your life is outweighed by what space exploration is going to bring, maybe not directly to your family, but to the world."[6]

The creative forces behind the possibilities of space exploration are the people—those who see beyond what is currently possible. We do not know what might be found out there, and the ISS will be used to discover the unknown. It will very likely be the greatest adventure of the twenty-first century.

Chapter Notes

Chapter 1. Danger in Space

1. Maia Weinstock, "Orbiting Junk Continues to Threaten International Space Station," *Space.com*, September 5, 2000, <http://www.space.com/scienceastronomy/planetearth/space_junk_000901.html> (October 24, 2003).
2. "USSTRATCOM Space Control and Space Surveillance," United States Strategic Command, December 2011, <http://www.stratcom.mil/factsheets/USSTRATCOM_Space_Control_and_Space_Surveillance/> (December 15, 2011).
3. Ibid.
4. Robert Coontz, Jr., "Space Junk," *Astronomy*, December 2000, vol. 28, issue 12, p. 56.
5. Robert Roy Britt, "Space Junk: The Stuff Left Behind," *Space.com*, October 19, 2000, <http://www.space.com/spacewatch/space_junk.html> (October 24, 2003).
6. Weinstock, "Orbiting Junk Continues to Threaten International Space Station."
7. NASA and Space.com Staff, "Space Junk FAQ: Falling Space Debris Explained," *Space.com*, September 9, 2011, <http://www.space.com/12894-space-debris-nasa-frequently-asked-questions.html> (December 15, 2011).

Chapter 2. Building the International Space Station

1. NASA, "International Space Station Assembly," NASA document LG-1999-09-522-HQ.
2. Mary F. Bell, "International Space Station: Turning Science Fiction Into Science Fact," NASA Facts, May 9, 2000, <http://www.hq.nasa.gov/office/pao/facts/HTML/FS-004-HQ.html> (October 24, 2003).
3. Kylie Moritz, "*Endeavour* Delivers Unity Node to International Space Station," STS-88, June 13, 2003, <http://spaceflight.nasa.gov/shuttle/archives/sts-88/index.html> (October 24, 2003).
4. Bill Shepherd, "Preflight Interview," *Human Spaceflight*, May 16, 2002, <http://spaceflight.nasa.gov/station/crew/exp1/intshepherd.html> (October 24, 2003).
5. Jason Quinn, NASA, e-mail to author, dated March 27, 2003.
6. Don Pettit, "Getting Ready for a Space Walk," *Space Station Science*, January 15, 2003, <http://science.nasa.gov/ppod/y2003/08apr_spacewalk.htm> (October 24, 2003).
7. *Inside the Space Station*, Discovery Channel Video, Discovery Channel Films, LLC, 2000.
8. Chris Culbert, "Robonaut Video Transcripts," *Video Transcripts*, March 19, 2001, <http://vesuvius.jsc.nasa.gov/er_er/html/robonaut/transcripts.htm#hand_motion> (October 24, 2003).
9. Richard Stenger, "'Robonaut' prepares for Spacewalking Duties," June 13, 2000, <http://cgi.cnn.com/2000/TECH/space/06/13/robonaut/index.html> (October 24, 2003).

10. Joe Bibby, "Robonaut (R2)," NASA, August 30, 2011, <http://robonaut.jsc.nasa.gov/default.asp> (January 16, 2012).

11. Glenn Research Center, "Powering the Future," NASA Facts FS-2000-11-006-GRC.

12. "Powering the Future," NASA Glenn Research Center, September 20, 2011, <http://www.nasa.gov/centers/glenn/about/fs06grc.html> (December 15, 2011).

13. Glenn Research Center, "Powering the Future."

Chapter 3. The First Space Stations

1. NASA, "International Space Station Assembly," NASA document LG-1999-09-522-HQ.

2. Sarah M. Murphy, "*Salyut 7* Space Station, Crews," *The Astronaut Connection,* February 8, 2000, <http://www.nauts.com/vehicles/80s/salyut7/index.html> (April 3, 2003).

3. Kylie Moritz, "Shuttle-*Mir* Background: Descriptions of *Mir*," History, September 17, 2003, <http://spaceflight.nasa.gov/history/shuttle-*Mir*/history/to-h-b-descriptions.htm> (October 24, 2003).

4. Kylie Moritz, "Mir's 15 Years," *Mir Space Station,* October 3, 2003, <http://spaceflight.nasa.gov/history/shuttle-mir/spacecraft/s-mir-15yrs-main.htm> (October 24, 2003).

5. John Uri, "ISS Risk Mitigation," *Shuttle-Mir History,* July 16, 1999, <http://spaceflight.nasa.gov/history/shuttle-mir/science/sc-iss.htm> (October 24, 2003).

6. NASA, "International Space Station Assembly."

7. Moritz, "Mir's 15 Years."

Chapter 4. Home Sweet Space Station

1. Jeff Hanley, "Mission Control Answers Your Questions," *NASA Human Spaceflight,* January 22, 2003, <http://spaceflight.nasa.gov/feedback/expert/answer/MCC/01_14_16_53_18.html> (October 24, 2003).

2. Ed Lu, "Ed Lu's Answers," *ISS Crew Answers: Expedition 7,* September 24, 2003, <http://spaceflight.nasa.gov/feedback/expert/answer/isscrew/index.html> (October 24, 2003).

3. Patrick Barry, "Wheels in the Sky," *Wheels in the Sky,* May 26, 2000, <http://science.nasa.gov/headlines/y2000/ast26may_1m.htm> (October 24, 2003).

4. Karen Miller, "Space Medicine," *Science@NASA,* September 30, 2002, <http://science.nasa.gov/headlines/y2002/30sept_spacemedicine.htm> (October 24, 2003).

5. John Curry, "Mission Control Answers Your Questions," *Human Spaceflight,* October 13, 2002, <http://spaceflight.nasa.gov/feedback/expert/answer/MCC/sts-112/09_12_09_40_34.html> (October 24, 2003).

6. Kylie Moritz, "Living in Space," *Human Spaceflight,* April 18, 2003, <http://spaceflight.nasa.gov/living/index.html> (October 24, 2003).

7. *Inside the Space Station,* Discovery Channel Video, Discovery Channel Films, LLC, 2000.

8. Jason Quinn, NASA, e-mail to author, dated March 27, 2003.

9. Patrick L. Barry and Tony Phillip, "Water on the Space Station: Making a Splash in Space," *Human Spaceflight,* April 18, 2003, <http://spaceflight.nasa.gov/living/factsheets/water2.html> (October 24, 2003).

10. Ibid.

11. Don Pettit, "Don Pettit's Answers," *ISS Crew Answers: Expedition Six,* May 1, 2003, <http://spaceflight.nasa.gov/feedback/expert/answer/isscrew/pettit2.html> (October 24, 2003).

12. Michael Mewhinney, "NASA Developing Autonomous Robot for Future Space Missions," *NASA Ames Research Center,* September 8, 1999, <http://amesnews.arc.nasa.gov/releases/1999/99_53AR.html> (April 3, 2003).

13. Jeff Jones, "Personal Satellite Assistant," *NASA Ames Research Center,* n.d., <http://ic.arc.nasa.gov/projects/psa/> (October 24, 2003).

14. Moritz, "Living in Space."

15. Rosemary Wilson, "Cures for Space Travelers," *New Science,* March 3, 2003, <http://liftoff.msfc.nasa.gov/news/2003/news-medicine.asp> (October 24, 2003).

Chapter 5. Research on the International Space Station

1. William R. Newcott, "Space Exploration: A Good Investment?" *National Geographic,* June 1999, <http://www.nationalgeographic.com/ngm/9906/forum/space-essay.html> (October 24, 2003).

2. NASA, "Research on the International Space Station," NASA document LG-1999-06-455-HQ.

3. *Inside the Space Station,* Discovery Channel Video, Discovery Channel Films, LLC, 2000.

4. Ibid.

5. Phil Davis, "Galileo," *Missions to Jupiter,* October 28, 2002, <http://solarsystem.nasa.gov/missions/jup_missns/jup-galileo.html> (October 24, 2003).

6. Dr. Tony Phillips and Steve Price, "Rocks in Your Gas Tank," *Science@NASA,* <http://science.nasa.gov/headlines/y2003/17apr_zeolite.htm?list893828> (October 24, 2003).

Chapter 6. Base Camp to the Universe

1. Dr. David P. Stern, "Gradual Acceleration by Low Thrust," *Far-out Pathways to Space: Solar Sails,* December 13, 2001, <http://wwwspof.gsfc.nasa.gov/stargaze/Solsail.htm> (October 24, 2003).

2. Joel Achenbach, "Life Beyond Earth," *National Geographic,* January 2000, p. 26.

3. Mike Schneider, "Psychologists Help Crew on International Space Station," *SpaceFlight,* February 21, 2003, <http://www.space.com/missionlaunches/iss_counsel_030221.html> (October 24, 2003).

4. Frank Morring, Jr., et al. "ISS: A New Crew of Two," *Aviation Week & Space Technology,* March 3, 2003, p. 24.

5. CBS News Coverage of Shuttle Mission STS–107, February 27, 2003.

6. Tony Reich, ed., *Space Shuttle—The First Twenty Years* (New York: DK Publishing, Inc., 2002), p. 274.

Glossary

cargo bay—Also called a payload bay, the central area of a space shuttle's fuselage in which payloads and their support equipment are carried.

centrifuge—A machine using centrifugal force for simulating gravitational effects.

microbe—A microorganism, especially a bacterium causing disease or fermentation.

microgravity—A condition in space in which only minuscule forces are experienced, or a virtual absence of gravity.

micrometeoroid—A microscopic particle in space that will not burn up if it enters Earth's atmosphere.

orbit—The circular path of one celestial body or artificial satellite around another.

photovoltaics—Utilizing the generation of a voltage when radiant energy falls on the boundary between dissimilar substances (as two different semiconductors).

Robonaut—A humanoid robot that performs work outside the International Space Station under the control of a human astronaut.

reentry—The phase of a spaceflight in which astronauts and their spacecraft first encounter Earth's atmosphere during their return from a mission.

space junk—The collection of objects in Earth orbit that were created by humans but no longer serve any useful purpose.

Further Reading

Books

Baker, David, and Heather Kissock. *International Space Station.* New York: Weigl Publishers, 2009.

Bortz, Fred. *Seven Wonders of Space Technology.* Minneapolis, Minn.: Twenty-First Century Books, 2011.

Rau, Dana Meachen. *The International Space Station.* Minneapolis, Minn.: Compass Point Books, 2005.

Skurzynski, Gloria. *This Is Rocket Science: True Stories of the Risk-Taking Scientists Who Figure Out Ways to Explore Beyond Earth.* Washington, D.C.: National Geographic, 2010.

Waxman, Laura Hamilton. *Exploring the International Space Station.* Minneapolis, Minn.: Lerner Publications, 2012.

Internet Addresses

Discovery.com: Inside the Space Station
<http://www.discovery.com/stories/science/iss/iss.html>

NASA: International Space Station
<http://www.nasa.gov/mission_pages/station/main/index.html>

USAToday.com: International Space Station 3-D Model
<http://i.usatoday.net/tech/graphics/iss_timeline/flash.htm>

Index